The 14th Amendment and the Incorporation Doctrine

The 14th Amendment and the Incorporation Doctrine

David Benner

Life & Liberty Publishing Group
Minneapolis, MN 55401

www.davebenner.com

ISBN: 0578189720
ISBN-13: 978-0578189727

Contents

Introduction   7

The Bill of Rights: Placing Limits on the   9
Federal Government

The Civil Rights Act of 1866   13

The Original Meaning of the 14th 15
Amendment

The Supreme Court Creates a New Doctrine   19

The Impact of Incorporation   23

Conclusion   29

Documents   33

About the Author   41

Notes   43

Introduction

Americans often describe their rights in terms of numbers derived from amendments in the federal Bill of Rights, an unambiguous set of limitations on government. Despite this tendency, most do not realize that such amendments were never designed to inhibit local authorities. Nevertheless, during the Progressive Era the federal courts began to claim that the 14th Amendment had "incorporated" federal Bill of Rights restrictions against the state governments. Ever since, this outlook has provided the basis upon which the federal judiciary overturns state laws deemed to be unsavory.

In a candid attempt to contradict the validity this phenomenon, this work aspires to establish that no such function was originally envisioned by the amendment. By demonstrating the subject's far-reaching ramifications, I also aim to illustrate how an absolute embrace of incorporation has severely eroded the Constitution's original intent. Without constitutional sanction, I will reveal how this fallacious doctrine has most often given the federal courts an excuse to meddle with the internal affairs of the states – a net negative for human liberty.

Today most Americans rely on the federal courts to sort out controversial and divisive matters, all the while believing that federal judges are above the inclinations of petty politicians. Still, the same judges that are granted such deference are actually well-connected lawyers, selected by presidents as unelected political appointees. They also carry similar academic backgrounds, proclivities concerning the orientation of the union, and theories on constitutional interpretation.

Today's Supreme Court, for example, consists of judges that represent two law schools. Without exception, all of them adhere to a whimsical legal system of *stare decisis* – judgment by precedent – rather than upholding the ratified constitutional understanding. Beyond this, they are almost uniformly inclined to uphold federal supremacy in all cases, even when such a position cannot be substantiated. Despite the philosophical differences between them, they all subscribe to the legitimacy of incorporation and its empowering effect on the federal courts.

For constitutional scholars, gaining a complete grasp on the 14th Amendment is a most mind-boggling and complicated journey. Without a doubt, the amendment is one of the most misunderstood aspects of the entire document. Despite this, its importance is amplified by the extent to which its long-lasting ramifications have affected the modern American political system. Almost every characteristic of contemporary legal theory is now a reaction to the way in which the federal courts have interpreted the 14th Amendment. In accordance with its analysis of one particular aspect of the amendment's reach, I hope this work will be redeeming to those who wish to gain a more clear understanding of the provision and its intended function. At the very least, I believe it will allay several myths and misconceptions regarding the 14th Amendment and the federal court's incorporation of the Bill of Rights.

More than anything else, I aim to show how the incorporation doctrine has led to the widespread annihilation of federalism, a chief maxim that was highly cherished by the founding generation. Paralleling this course, the incorporation mantra has also emboldened the centralization of judicial authority and political power in general. While the subject is virtually ignored in modern legal studies, the incorporation doctrine is now considered a settled matter of American jurisprudence. Despite the general lack of attention given to the topic, I remain adamant that no legal precept that has done more to transform the power of the federal judiciary into a superlative, harmful force, wholly detrimental to the interests of decentralized government.

The Bill of Rights: Placing Limits on the Federal Government

Before a deep study into the 14th Amendment and incorporation, it is important to understand that the limitations enumerated in the federal Bill of Rights weren't originally intended to act as prohibitions against the states. A careful reading of the preamble to the Bill of Rights instead makes clear that the amendments were added because the ratifying states sought to limit the scope of federal authority:

> "The Conventions of a number of the States, having at the time of their adopting the Constitution, expressed a desire, in order to prevent misconstruction or abuse of **its powers**, that further declaratory and restrictive clauses should be added: And as extending the ground of public confidence in the Government, will best ensure the beneficent ends of its institution."[Emphasis added]

Many of those that ratified the Constitution believed the new general government would usurp powers of the states without additional unambiguous prose. Because of this, many of the state ratifying conventions suggested specific amendments as a way to make these principles overt, and insisted on their inclusion as a condition of ratification.

None of the state ratification ordinances included language asserting that any proposed amendment would inhibit any state powers, nor those of their fellow states. However, the states did include text that articulated their wishes that amendments provide explicit limitations against the **federal** authority. For instance, Massachusetts' 1788 ratification ordinance clarified definitively which government was to be limited by the proposed amendments:

> "And as it is the opinion of this convention that certain amendments and alterations in the said Constitution would remove the fears, and quiet the apprehensions of many of the good people of this commonwealth, and more effectually guard against an undue administration **of the federal government** - The convention do therefore recommend that the following alterations and provisions be introduced into the said Constitution."[Emphasis added].[1]

Similarly, New Hampshire's ratification document echoed this sentiment verbatim.[2]

New York's ratification instrument mentioned that many fears concerning ratification would be allayed if specific amendments were adopted. The document went on to list the proposals, all of which designated only Congress as the body to be inhibited by the proposals. A cursory reading of the ratification announcements from all states demonstrates the same phenomenon, and no state proposed supplemental limitations upon its own sovereign power.

In the First Congress, James Madison initially proposed amendment language stating "that no state shall violate the equal right of conscience, freedom of the press, or trial by jury in criminal cases; because it is proper that every government should be disarmed of powers which trench upon those particular rights." This proposal, which would have placed such limitation expressly upon the states, was rejected.[3] Additionally, the amendments were written in a way to leave no confusion about which entity would be impeded by the dictums. This is revealed through the text of the First Amendment: "Congress shall make no law…" makes the focal point of the limitations unmistakable.

The most resounding evidence that can be used to illustrate this is the fact that many of the state governments retained official state churches long into the 19th century. Connecticut, for instance, recognized the Congressionalist church as its official state religion until 1818. Massachusetts discontinued funding for its state church only in 1833. During this time, no one in the general government challenged the legitimacy of such arrangements on the basis that the First Amendment disallowed their existence. Instead, this understanding of the Bill of Rights limitations was universally recognized.

For the first time, in 1833, a suit against the state of Maryland alleged that the Fifth Amendment right to due process extended to inhibit the state governments. In *Barron v. Baltimore,* the John Marshall Court correctly held that the amendments did no such thing – they only limited the federal government. Despite his typical arch-nationalist penchants, a Marshall's reasoning beautifully captures the intended structure of the American political system:

"The constitution was ordained and established by the people of the United States for themselves, for their own government, and not for the government of the individual states. Each state established a constitution for itself, and in that constitution, provided such limitations and restrictions on the powers of its particular government, as its judgment dictated. The people of the United States framed such a government for the United States as they supposed best adapted to their situation and best calculated to promote their interests. The powers they conferred on this government were to be exercised by itself; and the limitations on power, if expressed in general terms, are naturally, and, we think, necessarily, applicable to the government created by the instrument. They are limitations of power granted in the instrument itself; not of distinct governments, framed by different persons and for different purposes...If these propositions be correct, the fifth amendment must be understood as restraining the power of the general government, not as applicable to the states. In their several constitutions, they have imposed such restrictions on their respective governments, as their own wisdom suggested; such as they deemed most proper for themselves. It is a subject on which they judge exclusively, and with which others interfere no further than they are supposed to have a common interest."[4]

By this reasoning, John Barron failed to win his suit against Maryland. After the opinion, Marshall's conclusion went unchallenged for almost 100 years.

The Civil Rights Act of 1866

After the Civil War, Congress passed legislation to ensure newly freed slaves enjoyed the same basic fundamental rights and privileges as their white counterparts. The legislation became known as The Civil Rights Act of 1866. The law was constructed to enumerate very specific objects, all of which affirmed that all freedmen possessed the following inherent rights:

"To make and enforce contracts, to sue, be parties, and give evidence, to inherit, purchase, lease, sell, hold, and convey real and personal property, and to full and equal benefit of all laws and proceedings for the security of person and property, as is enjoyed by white citizens, and shall be subject to like punishment, pains, and penalties, and to none other, any law, statute, ordinance, regulation, or custom, to the contrary notwithstanding."[5]

In hindsight, most of these are freedoms that most Americans would consider assumptive and obvious. Among them is the right to engage in purchases, own property, and to guarantee that the terms of a contract would be fulfilled. In the contemporary, nobody would question a person's right to enter into contracts, own property, and access the courts. However, at that time, many blacks remained in a state of de-facto slavery, denied even these most basic rights.

This act became incredibly controversial because of its constitutional ramifications. Since it interfered with powers reserved to the states, and conferred citizenship at a time where 11 states remained unrepresented in Congress, President Andrew Johnson vetoed the bill. This act was met with sincere scrutiny, and Congress successfully overrode the veto. Subsequently, the bill became law on April 9, 1866.

Despite the adoption of the law through a veto override, the act faced immense opposition. Many of its advocates claimed the law would simply be repealed when the Democrats next took power, or negated by the federal courts when it took up disputes concerning the constitutionality of related suits. When these uncertainties became evident, Republicans decided to draft a constitutional amendment to constitutionalize its passage. This decision led to the inception of the 14th Amendment.

When southern states initially refused to ratify the amendment, the State Department under William Seward passed a decree that made state representation in the federal government conditional upon whether a state ratified the amendment or not. When several states remained defiant against the mandate, the federal government established military governments in the southern states. These non-republican military governments claimed sovereignty over those states and ratified the amendment by force. Although many modern legal scholars contend otherwise, numerous historians persuasively argue that the 14th Amendment was never legitimately ratified.[6]

The Original Meaning of the 14ᵗʰ Amendment

In the contemporary, most portions of the 14ᵗʰ Amendment are not especially controversial. One provision prevented Confederates from representing a state in the federal government unless Congress removed the restriction – which was eventually accomplished on a great scale in the following years. Another delegitimized the assumption of the debts incurred by the Confederate States of America and southern states as part of the war.

The first part of Section 1 of the 14ᵗʰ Amendment explicitly negates the Supreme Court decision in *Scott v. Sandford*, which opined that blacks, whether slave or free, could not be considered as American citizens:

> "All persons born or naturalized in the United States, and subject to the jurisdiction thereof, are citizens of the United States and of the State wherein they reside."

The next part is at the root of the contemporary legal transformation of the amendment:

> "No State shall make or enforce any law which shall abridge the privileges or immunities of citizens of the United States; nor shall any State deprive any person of life, liberty, or property, without due process of law; nor deny to any person within its jurisdiction the equal protection of the laws."

The chief purpose of this passage, and the 14ᵗʰ Amendment in general, was to affirm the new freedmen the same due process rights as their whites and to constitutionalize the Civil Rights Act of 1866. A key proponent of the amendment, West Virginia Representative George Latham said that the

Civil Rights Act "covers exactly the same ground as the amendment."[7] Senator Lyman Trumbull, who made painstaking strides to ensure the bill's passage, recognized the function of the act to be "a reiteration of the rights as set forth in the Civil Rights Bill."[8] On several occasions, Trumbull stated that the Civil Rights bill had no application to a state that did not discriminate between its citizens on these grounds. Senator John Sherman of Ohio even remarked that "the first section was an embodiment of the [Civil Rights] Act."[9]

Regarding "equal protection under the law" – a passage that gets much attention – if the right was not afforded to a white citizen in 1866, it wasn't expected to be furnished to anyone according to the amendment's advocates. For example, the federal government did not intend to use this text to affirm the right of women to vote in any state that denied female suffrage. Similarly, the law did not empower the federal courts to suddenly overturn state laws that prevented individuals under the age of 18 from voting.

Alternative applications of either the Civil Rights Act or the amendment were never revealed or accepted in the debates. In his groundbreaking work on the subject, *Government by Judiciary: the Transformation of the Fourteenth Amendment*, historian and constitutional scholar Raoul Berger summed this up in the following way:

> "If there was a concealed intention to go beyond the Civil Rights Act, it was not ratified because, first, ratification requires disclosure of material facts, whereas there was no disclosure that the Amendment was meant to uproot, for example, traditional State judicial procedures and practices; and, second, a surrender of recognized rights may not be presumed but must be proved."[10]

In cases which followed on the heels of the 14th Amendment, the federal courts continued to hold that the Bill of Rights did not apply to state action, and federal opinions failed to mention the amendment at all.[11] Simply put, passage of the 14th Amendment did not overturn or override the implicit principle, or the explicit verbiage codified in the Tenth Amendment, that all powers that the states did not delegate to the federal government were reserved to the states and the people.

Another episode that challenges the legitimacy of the incorporation doctrine can be found in a failed attempt to apply Bill of Rights limitations to the states. Senator James Blaine of Maine proposed an amendment to the Constitution in 1875 that would apply the First Amendment restrictions upon the states. The proposal died in the House of Representatives, failing to achieve the two-thirds vote necessary to be sent to the states for adoption. If the 14th Amendment did what the federal courts now say it did, Blaine's proposal would have been unneeded and irrelevant.

A casual read of Section 1 does not seem especially provocative or contentious. However, today's federal judiciary now cites this part of the amendment to justify incorporation, or the theory that the federal Bill of Rights now applies as restrictions against the state governments as well as the federal government. This legal theory has become known as the "incorporation doctrine." Despite this radical judicial transformation, Berger wrote that "no such purpose was entertained" by the ratification of the 14th Amendment.[12]

The Supreme Court Creates a
New Doctrine

While most legal scholars accept it as an undeniable truth, application of the Bill of Rights to the states through the 14th Amendment was not always an accepted doctrine. In fact, the federal judiciary did not claim the amendment had this effect until more than 55 years after ratification. In the pivotal Slaughter-House Cases of the 1870s, the Supreme Court specifically rejected the notion that the text applied the Bill of Rights to the state authorities:

"Was it the purpose of the fourteenth amendment, by the simple declaration that no State should make or enforce any law which shall abridge the privileges and immunities of citizens of the United States, to transfer the security and protection of all the civil rights which we have mentioned, from the States to the Federal government? And where it is declared that Congress Shall have the power to enforce that article, was it intended to bring within the power of Congress the entire domain of civil rights heretofore belonging exclusively to the States? We are convinced that no such results were intended by the Congress which proposed these amendments, nor by the legislatures of the States which ratified them."[13]

This was the only persuasion held by the federal judiciary for the next several decades. In fact, this understanding was affirmed in the 1922 case of *Prudential Insurance Company of America v. Cheek*, which concerned New York's ability to restrict freedom of speech. In this case, the majority opinion repeated this concept:

"But, as we have stated, neither the Fourteenth Amendment nor any other provision of the Constitution of the United States imposes upon the states any restrictions about 'freedom of speech' or the 'liberty of silence'; nor, we may add, does it confer any right of privacy upon either persons or corporations."[14]

It was only in 1925 that the federal judiciary magically discovered that Section 1 of the 14th Amendment had the effect of incorporation. For over 50 years prior, the idea that the codicil had no such effect was all but a universal legal creed.

Even by the mid-20th century, when the incorporation doctrine had become fully embraced by the federal judiciary, some justices remained honest concerning the original intent of the 14th Amendment. In a dissent to the 1938 case of *Connecticut General Life Insurance Company v. Johnson*, Supreme Court Justice Hugo Black wrote the following:

"The states did not adopt the Amendment with knowledge of its sweeping meaning under its present construction. No section of the Amendment gave notice to the people that, if adopted, it would subject every state law...affecting [judicial processes]...to censorship of the United States courts. No word in all this Amendment gave any hint that its adoption would deprive the states of their long recognized power to regulate [judicial processes]."[15]

In the 1959 case of *Bartkus v. Illinois*, Supreme Court Justice Felix Frankfurter correctly pontificated:

"We have held from the beginning and uniformly that the Due Process Clause of the Fourteenth Amendment does not apply to the States any of the provisions of the first eight amendments as such. The relevant historical materials have been canvassed by this Court and by legal scholars. These materials demonstrate conclusively that Congress and the members of the legislatures of the ratifying States did not contemplate that the Fourteenth Amendment was a short-hand incorporation of the first eight amendments making them applicable as explicit restrictions upon the States."[16]

Although lingering attitudes challenging the incorporation doctrine continued to linger throughout the 20th century, as a matter of judicial theory the issue was considered settled. Because it was deemed convenient, the federal judiciary arbitrarily expanded its own authority through an unsubstantiated legal theory.

The Impact of Incorporation

Rejecting the original understanding, contemporary misapplication of the incorporation doctrine serves as a catalyst for the federal judiciary to exploit and abuse the states. In modern application, this dogma has been used to justify a whole host of new "rights" that are usually privileges paid for by one class and distributed to others through governmental force. The notion that the 14th Amendment intended to bring about these privileges through modern jurisprudential misapplication is demonstrably ludicrous.

Since the 1920s, federal judges have used the incorporation doctrine as rationalization to:

- Ensure the expansion of state welfare systems according to the wishes through *Goldberg v. Kelly*. In this case, the Court held that the Due Process Clause of the 14th Amendment guaranteed the "right" to welfare benefits.

- Decide, in the 2008 case of *Kennedy v. Louisiana*, that criminals who rape children have the constitutional right to evade execution through incorporation of the Eighth Amendment.

- Determine that local governments could seize land from individuals and provide it to private entities. We find this opinion in the 2005 case of *Kelo v. City of New London*, where the Supreme Court decided that the incorporation of the Takings Clause of the Fifth Amendment allowed local governments to engage in such behavior.

- Announce, in the 1923 case of *Meyer v. Nebraska,* that all Americans had the "constitutional right" to learn German based on the incorporation doctrine. The Supreme Court forcibly prevented the state from altering its own educational curriculum.

- Contend, via the 1989 case of *County of Allegheny v. American Civil Liberties Union*, that the display of a menorah in downtown Pittsburgh was constitutional, while a Christian nativity scene in the same area was unconstitutional.

- Opine, through the 2005 case of *McCreary County v. ACLU of Kentucky,* that a display of the Ten Commandments at a courthouse was a violation of the Establishment Clause, which according to the court was incorporated through the 14th Amendment

- Declare, in the 1968 case of *Epperson v. Arkansas,* that state schools must tailor their theistic studies to the interests of the federal government.

- Profess, through the 1975 case of *Gross v. Lopez*, that public schools must conduct federally-structured hearings prior to subjecting a student to a suspension.

- Establish, through the 1973 case of *Roe v. Wade,* that federal due process through the 14th Amendment prohibited the states from upholding their own systems of criminal law, malignantly encroaching upon their reserved authority under the Constitution.

- Decide, through the 1941 case of *Edwards v. California,* that the state must pay welfare to nonresident "indigent persons" on 14th Amendment grounds. California had enacted a statute limiting welfare benefits in order to decrease a bloated budget, but the court invalidated the statute and forced it to expand its welfare system.

Even when the federal judiciary intervenes in matters reserved to the states to protect individual liberty, the judges often reserve the authority to impose arbitrary restrictions and regulations concerning the rights in question. For example, this occurred in the 1925 case of *Gitlow v. New York*. In that matter, the court announced that the 14th Amendment prohibited the states from infringing upon an individual's free speech, but opined that such a right could not be utilized to challenge the legitimacy of a government or advocate an overthrow.

The same phenomenon has also unfolded in the 2008 case of *District of Columbia v. Heller*, where the Supreme Court maintained that the Second Amendment affirmed the right to keep and bear arms, but made the following restrictive decree against firearm ownership:

> "Like most rights, the Second Amendment right is not unlimited. It is not a right to keep and carry any weapon whatsoever in any manner whatsoever and for whatever purpose: For example, concealed weapons prohibitions have been upheld under the Amendment or state analogues. The Court's opinion should not be taken to cast doubt on longstanding prohibitions on the possession of firearms by felons and the mentally ill, or laws forbidding the carrying of firearms in sensitive places such as schools and government buildings, or laws imposing conditions and qualifications on the commercial sale of arms. Miller's holding that the sorts of weapons protected are those "in common use at the time" finds support in the historical tradition of prohibiting the carrying of dangerous and unusual weapons."[17]

While it may surprise some readers, this opinion was written by Antonin Scalia, widely considered as one of the most pro-gun federal judges in recent memory. If nothing else, this episode demonstrates that no federal judge can be trusted with a sincere view of the amendment's purpose. While acting to incorporate the restriction, the high court inserted a caveat for the future erosion of a natural right.

Scalia's position in *Heller* is historically unfounded – the Second Amendment was constructed to prevent the federal government from even so much as approaching the idea of rules or regulations on gun ownership, voiding the potential for any restrictive firearm legislation.[18] The founders were accordingly wise enough to embrace federalism and rely on the states to determine these matters for themselves. If a state carried its own policy to undesirable ends, the people within that state could simply migrate with impunity, or impose restrictions on their own state governments through constitutional amendments. Through these types of decisions, the federal courts have systematically negated founding doctrine and supplanted state law with edicts that are passed down from a nine-member oligarchy.

Recent history has proved that deference to the federal judiciary ultimately impedes liberty, since federal judges don't share valid or genuine conceptions of liberty. This fact can be illustrated through the recent comments of a very influence federal judge. At an American Bar Association luncheon, retired Supreme Court Justice John Paul Stevens said the following:

> "I endorse the Court's holding that the Due Process Clause of the 14th Amendment protects an individual's right to choose his or her spouse but I remain unpersuaded that that Clause also protects an individual's right to use a gun. The dissenters have things backward when they argue that it protects the latter but not the former.".[19]

On face value, this is a perplexing claim – the right to keep and bear arms is affirmed explicitly in the Bill of Rights, while civil unions and religious sacraments are not. In overt fashion, the Tenth Amendment of the Constitution reserves all powers not enumerated in the document to the states or the people. Quoting the amendment directly, Thomas Jefferson wrote in 1791 that "the foundation of the Constitution [was] laid on this ground.".[20]

To suggest that a prohibition which is unambiguously spelled out in the Bill of Rights is not incorporated, while a power that was reserved to the states is, would boggle the mind of the most biased observer. In hindsight, even those with good intentions who support the incorporation doctrine should now acknowledge the transparent actuality – federal judges just don't get it. Instead of candidly enforcing original intent, they usually rule by preference. Even if incorporation was a legitimate, constitutional canon, this situation reveals that we cannot trust federal judges to faithfully uphold it.

Although some federal judges have expressed doubt on the validity of the incorporation doctrine, such opinions are often glossed over or ignored entirely. For instance, former federal judge and Supreme Court nominee Robert Bork wrote that the incorporation doctrine inappropriately expanded the Supreme Court's power and threatened federalism. Tellingly, he also decried the extent to which the federal courts had overridden judicial interpretations of the states. "That meant making its interpretations of the various amendments the uniform law throughout the nation, which had never occurred before," Bork wrote..[21]

Conclusion

In *Compact of the Republic: The League of States and the Constitution*, I wrote of the destructive influence of the incorporation doctrine on the development of American jurisprudence:

> "While the incorporation doctrine has sometimes acted to preserve individual liberty, in most cases it is just used as a federal excuse to meddle in the business of state law. It has given federal judges the ability to interject their own opinions into state issues, provides the federal government a pretext for policing the entities that built it, and allows the federal courts to redefine rights in a way that it was never meant to...it has made the federal judiciary into a nationalist, untouchable branch of government."[22]

Undoubtedly, the widespread adoption of this dogma has had far-reaching implications. Nonetheless, through the conditioning of government education, exposure to media narratives, and a general trend toward nationalism in the United States, regular Americans are largely unaware of its boundless influence in their everyday lives.

While I often justify my political opinions based on the constitutionality of a policy, let's take that out of the equation for a moment. An honest observer may ask, is the incorporation doctrine good for the continuance of human liberty and the preservation of inalienable rights? If we truly believe in individual rights, shouldn't we welcome any such inhibitions against state governments? I think the answer to these questions lies in the fallibility of government officials. If we were ruled by failsafe angels of liberty that shared the same notions of liberty as the American founders, I believe the answer may be yes. If federal judges read and understood the Constitution in the same way I do, I might be willing to concede that they could suitably act to contravene tangible infringements on individual rights.

However, the sad and obvious fact is that federal judges have no such predilections. We are not governed by angels that understand human liberty; far from it. If the federal judges cannot fail to see how the NSA surveillance program or federal firearm restrictions are complete violations of constitutionally recognized rights, how can we trust them to sort such things out at the state level, or pinpoint state violations? Realistically, they can't and won't. More often, judges simply use the incorporation doctrine to interfere with powers the founders wished to be reserved to the state governments. Instead of protecting individual rights, federal judges more often base their opinions on personal proclivities.

Instead of subscribing to the fantasy that federal judges are infallible interpreters of the Constitution, James Madison articulated the reality in *The Federalist* #51. Therein, he explicitly remarked that all men are not angels, especially men in government. They cannot be expected to carry out their duties perfectly and without partiality or preference. Moreover, they are susceptible to the inclinations of prestige, power, and corruption.

When federal justices are given the unrivaled power to intervene in local matters, we shouldn't be taken back by the results. The federal courts almost never side with states over federal authority, and the overextension of judicial authority allows federal judges inject their own views into local matters. Additionally, it provides small councils of powerful judges the ability to make their opinions uniformly binding upon 320 million people. Through the incorporation doctrine, we have reached an ultimate political inversion – where powerful judges are permitted to change the purpose of 14th Amendment to meet any whimsical political desire. As long as it encourages a desired political end, no can mean yes and yes can mean no.

If the incorporation doctrine is embraced to the fullest extent, it would also render the need for state bills of rights irrelevant. Do its advocates really expect us to believe that a person's right to keep and bear arms and assert grievances against government began only in 1791? At that point, many states had explicit affirmations of such rights that pre-dated the federal counterparts. Until the 1830s, many had official state religions. The idea that the federal bill of rights should supersede and override the state counterparts is as big of a blow against federalism as any other form of government overreach.

By no surprise, the incorporation doctrine has a huge effect on legal education and law curriculum. Today, most lawyers concentrate their studies on federal law over state law at a highly disproportionate rate, with the implicit understanding that state law can ultimately be negated by the federal judiciary. In constructing strategy to build cases, these attorneys often appeal to the high courts to overturn the supposed faulty decisions of their own local courts. By doing so, they empower the federal judiciary and the oligarchy it has become to an astonishing degree.

Ultimately, local courts are far closer to the interests of the parties involved in the disputes. Although not perfect, state judicial systems are more than adequate to interpret and apply state law to local disputes. These factors work together to make state courts the proper forums for the consideration of local cases. Additionally, many state judges are chosen through republican elections, and are much more closely tied to the interests of individuals.

Those who celebrate when a federal court interposes their own opinions on controversial local matters may be deeply saddened in due time. If the federal courts can rule simply by decree, their actions will ultimately serve as precedents for the further consolidation of power. At some point, those who find favor with the edicts of today will certainly be oppressed by those that come tomorrow.

Documents

The 14th Amendment to the United States Constitution

Section 1. All persons born or naturalized in the United States, and subject to the jurisdiction thereof, are citizens of the United States and of the State wherein they reside. No State shall make or enforce any law which shall abridge the privileges or immunities of citizens of the United States; nor shall any State deprive any person of life, liberty, or property, without due process of law; nor deny to any person within its jurisdiction the equal protection of the laws.

Section 2. Representatives shall be apportioned among the several States according to their respective numbers, counting the whole number of persons in each State, excluding Indians not taxed. But when the right to vote at any election for the choice of electors for President and Vice President of the United States, Representatives in Congress, the Executive and Judicial officers of a State, or the members of the Legislature thereof, is denied to any of the male inhabitants of such State, being twenty-one years of age, and citizens of the United States, or in any way abridged, except for participation in rebellion, or other crime, the basis of representation therein shall be reduced in the proportion which the number of such male citizens shall bear to the whole number of male citizens twenty-one years of age in such State.

Section 3. No person shall be a Senator or Representative in Congress, or elector of President and Vice President, or hold any office, civil or military, under the United States, or under any State, who, having previously taken an oath, as a member of Congress, or as an officer of the United States, or as a member of any State legislature, or as an executive or judicial officer of any State, to support the Constitution of the United States, shall have engaged in insurrection or rebellion against the same, or given aid or comfort to the enemies thereof. But Congress may, by a vote of two-thirds of each House, remove such disability.

Section 4. The validity of the public debt of the United States, authorized by law, including debts incurred for payment of pensions and bounties for services in suppressing insurrection or rebellion, shall not be questioned. But neither the United States nor any State shall assume or pay any debt or obligation incurred in aid of insurrection or rebellion against the United States, or any claim for the loss or emancipation of any slave; but all such debts, obligations and claims shall be held illegal and void.

Section 5. The Congress shall have power to enforce, by appropriate legislation, the provisions of this article.

The Civil Rights Act of 1866

An Act to protect all Persons in the United States in their Civil Rights, and furnish the Means of their Vindication.

Be it enacted by the Senate and House of Representatives of the United States of America in Congress assembled, That all persons born in the United States and not subject to any foreign power, excluding Indians not taxed, are hereby declared to be citizens of the United States; and such citizens, of every race and color, without regard to any previous condition of slavery or involuntary servitude, except as a punishment for crime whereof the party shall have been duly convicted, shall have the same right, in every State and Territory in the United States, to make and enforce contracts, to sue, be parties, and give evidence, to inherit, purchase, lease, sell, hold, and convey real and personal property, and to full and equal benefit of all laws and proceedings for the security of person and property, as is enjoyed by white citizens, and shall be subject to like punishment, pains, and penalties, and to none other, any law, statute, ordinance, regulation, or custom, to the contrary notwithstanding.

Sec. 2. And be it further enacted, That any person who, under color of any law, statute, ordinance, regulation, or custom, shall subject, or cause to be subjected, any inhabitant of any State or Territory to the deprivation of any right secured or protected by this act, or to different punishment, pains, or penalties on account of such person having at any time been held in a condition of slavery or involuntary servitude, except as a punishment for crime whereof the party shall have been duly convicted, or by reason of his color or race, than is prescribed for the punishment of white persons, shall be deemed guilty of a misdemeanor, and, on conviction, shall be punished by fine not exceeding one thousand dollars, or imprisonment not exceeding one year, or both, in the discretion of the court.

Sec. 3. And be it further enacted, That the district courts of the United States, within their respective districts, shall have, exclusively of the courts of the several States, cognizance of all crimes and offences committed against the provisions of this act, and also, concurrently with the circuit courts of the United States, of all causes, civil and criminal, affecting persons who are denied or cannot enforce in the courts or judicial tribunals of the State or locality where they may be any of the rights secured to them by the first section of this act; and if any suit or prosecution, civil or criminal, has been or shall be commenced in any State court, against any such person, for any cause whatsoever, or against any officer, civil or military, or other person, for any arrest or imprisonment, trespasses, or wrongs done or committed by virtue or under color of authority derived from this act or the act establishing a Bureau for the relief of Freedmen and Refugees, and all acts amendatory thereof, or for refusing to do any act upon the ground that it would be inconsistent with this act, such defendant shall have the right to remove such cause for trial to the proper district or circuit court in the manner prescribed by the "Act relating to habeas corpus and regulating judicial proceedings in certain cases," approved March three, eighteen hundred and sixty-three, and all acts amendatory thereof. The jurisdiction in civil and criminal matters hereby conferred on the district and circuit courts of the United States shall be exercised and enforced in conformity with the laws of the United States, so far as such laws are suitable to carry the same into effect; but in all cases where such laws are not adapted to the object, or are deficient in the provisions necessary to furnish suitable remedies and punish offences against law, the common law, as modified and changed by the constitution and statutes of the State wherein the court having jurisdiction of the cause, civil or criminal, is held, so far as the same is not inconsistent with the Constitution and laws of the United States, shall be extended to and govern said courts in the trial and disposition of such cause, and, if of a criminal nature, in the infliction of punishment on the party found guilty.

Sec. 4. And be it further enacted, That the district attorneys, marshals, and deputy marshals of the United States, the commissioners appointed by the circuit and territorial courts of the United States, with powers of arresting, imprisoning, or bailing offenders against the laws of the United States, the officers and agents of the Freedmen's Bureau, and every other officer who may be specially empowered by the President of the United States, shall be, and they are hereby, specially authorized and required, at the expense of the United States, to institute proceedings against all and every person who shall violate the provisions of this act, and cause him or them to be arrested and imprisoned, or bailed, as the case may be, for trial before such court of the United States or territorial court as by this act has cognizance of the offence. And with a view to affording reasonable protection to all persons in their constitutional rights of equality before the law, without distinction of race or color, or previous condition of slavery or involuntary servitude, except as a punishment for crime, whereof the party shall have been duly convicted, and to the prompt discharge of the duties of this act, it shall be the duty of the circuit courts of the United States and the superior courts of the Territories of the United States, from time to time, to increase the number of commissioners, so as to afford a speedy and convenient means for the arrest and examination of persons charged with a violation of this act; and such commissioners are hereby authorized and required to exercise and discharge all the powers and duties conferred on them by this act, and the same duties with regard to offences created by this act, as they are authorized by law to exercise with regard to other offences against the laws of the United States.

Sec. 5. And be it further enacted, That it shall be the duty of all marshals and deputy marshals to obey and execute all warrants and precepts issued under the provisions of this act, when to them directed; and should any marshal or deputy marshal refuse to receive such warrant or other process when tendered, or to use all proper means diligently to execute the same, he shall, on conviction thereof, be fined in the sum of one thousand dollars, to the use of the person upon whom the accused is alleged to have committed the offense. And the better to enable the said commissioners to execute their duties faithfully and efficiently, in conformity with the Constitution of the United States and the requirements of this act, they are hereby authorized and empowered, within their counties respectively, to appoint, in writing, under their hands, any one or more suitable persons, from time to time, to execute all such warrants and other process as may be issued by them in the lawful performance of their respective duties; and the persons so appointed to execute any warrant or process as aforesaid shall have authority to summon and call to their aid the bystanders or posse comitatus of the proper county, or such portion of the land or naval forces of the United States, or of the militia, as may be necessary to the performance of the duty with which they are charged, and to insure a faithful observance of the clause of the Constitution which prohibits slavery, in conformity with the provisions of this act; and said warrants shall run and be executed by said officers anywhere in the State or Territory within which they are issued.

Sec. 6. And be it further enacted, That any person who shall knowingly and wilfully obstruct, hinder, or prevent any officer, or other person charged with the execution of any warrant or process issued under the provisions of this act, or any person or persons lawfully assisting him or them, from arresting any person for whose apprehension such warrant or process may have been issued, or shall rescue or attempt to rescue such person from the custody of the officer, other person or persons, or those lawfully assisting as aforesaid, when so arrested pursuant to the authority herein given and declared, or shall aid, abet, or assist any person so arrested as aforesaid, directly or indirectly, to escape from the custody of the officer or other person legally authorized as aforesaid, or shall harbor or conceal any person for whose arrest a warrant or process shall have been issued as aforesaid, so as to prevent his discovery and arrest after notice or knowledge of the fact that a warrant has been issued for the apprehension of such person, shall, for either of said offences, be subject to a fine not exceeding one thousand dollars, and imprisonment not exceeding six months, by indictment and conviction before the district court of the United States for the district in which said offense may have been committed, or before the proper court of criminal jurisdiction, if committed within any one of the organized Territories of the United States.

Sec. 7. And be it further enacted, That the district attorneys, the marshals, their deputies, and the clerks of the said district and territorial courts shall be paid for their services the like fees as may be allowed to them for similar services in other cases; and in all cases where the proceedings are before a commissioner, he shall be entitled to a fee of ten dollars in full for his services in each case, inclusive of all services incident to such arrest and examination. The person or persons authorized to execute the process to be issued by such commissioners for the arrest of offenders against the provisions of this act shall be entitled to a fee of five dollars for each person he or they may arrest and take before any such commissioner as aforesaid, with such other fees as may be deemed reasonable by such commissioner for such other additional services as may be necessarily performed by him or them, such as attending at the examination, keeping the prisoner in custody, and providing him with food and lodging during his detention, and until the final determination of such commissioner, and in general for performing such other duties as may be required in the premises; such fees to be made up in conformity with the fees usually charged by the officers of the courts of justice within the proper district or county, as near as may be practicable, and paid out of the Treasury of the United States on the certificate of the judge of the district within which the arrest is made, and to be recoverable from the defendant as part of the judgment in case of conviction.

Sec. 8. And be it further enacted, That whenever the President of the United States shall have reason to believe that offences have been or are likely to be committed against the provisions of this act within any judicial district, it shall be lawful for him, in his discretion, to direct the judge, marshal, and district attorney of such district to attend at such place within the district, and for such time as he may designate, for the purpose of the more speedy arrest and trial of persons charged with a violation of this act; and it shall be the duty of every judge or other officer, when any such requisition shall be received by him, to attend at the place and for the time therein designated.

Sec. 9. And be it further enacted, That it shall be lawful for the President of the United States, or such person as he may empower for that purpose, to employ such part of the land or naval forces of the United States, or of the militia, as shall be necessary to prevent the violation and enforce the due execution of this act.

Sec. 10. And be it further enacted, That upon all questions of law arising in any cause under the provisions of this act a final appeal may be taken to the Supreme Court of the United States.

SCHUYLER COLFAX,
Speaker of the House of Representatives.

LAFAYETTE S. FOSTER,
President of the Senate, pro tempore.

In the Senate of the United States, April 6, 1866.

The President of the United States having returned to the Senate, in which it originated, the bill entitled "An act to protect all persons in the United States in their civil rights, and furnish the means of their vindication," with his objections thereto, the Senate proceeded, in pursuance of the Constitution, to reconsider the same; and,

Resolved, That the said bill do pass, two-thirds of the Senate agreeing to pass the same.

Attest:

J.W. Forney,
Secretary of the Senate.

In the House of Representatives U.S. April 9th, 1866.

The House of Representatives having proceeded, in pursuance of the Constitution, to reconsider the bill entitled, "An act to protect all persons in the United States in their civil rights, and furnish the means of their vindication," returned to the Senate by the President of the United States, with his objections, and sent by the Senate to the House of Representatives, with the message of the President returning the bill:

Resolved, That the bill do pass, two-thirds of the House of Representatives agreeing to pass the same.

Attest:

EDWARD MCPHERSONE, Clerk,

by CLINTON LLOYD, Chief Clerk

About the Author

David Benner speaks regularly in Minnesota on topics related to the United States Constitution, founding principles, and United States history. He contributes articles to The Tenth Amendment Center, Abbeville Institute, Intellectual Takeout, and several local publications. He is also the author of *Compact of the Republic: The League of States and the Constitution*, which throws a wrench into the wheel of contemporary legal thought by depicting the Constitution as a compact between the several states.

David adheres to the compact view of the Constitution espoused by Thomas Jefferson and James Madison. He recognizes that the Constitution was not ratified by "one people," but by several distinctly sovereign entities, which by state ratification gave the Constitution legally binding status. David actively denies and refutes modern understandings of the Constitution made long after the ratification conventions, which claim that the Constitution is a "living document" that grants the federal government a vast reservoir of "implied" powers.

David considers himself as Jeffersonian at heart and teaches about the dangers of an overreaching centralized authority, viewing the states as the "surest bulwarks against antirepublican tendencies." He is an opponent of perpetual debt, centralized banking, and fiat currency, and uses constitutional arguments in support of these positions.

David was born in Knoxville, Tennessee, and has lived most of his life in Minnesota and Wisconsin. He has a Bachelor's Degree in History Education from the University of Wisconsin, River Falls. He currently resides in Roseville, Minnesota.

Notes

[1] Ratification of the Commonwealth of Massachusetts, in *The Debates in the Several State Conventions on the Adoption of the Federal Constitution,* Edited by Jonathan Elliot (Washington: Taylor & Maury, 1861), Volume I, 354.

[2] Ibid, 358.

[3] Debates in Congress, Amendments to the Constitution, June 8, 1789, in *The Debates and Proceedings in the Congress of the United States* (Washington: Gales and Seaton, 1834), Volume I, 457. After being rejected, Madison's attempt to incorporate speech, press, and religious protections against the states failed to appear in his second draft of the Bill of Rights.

[4] Barron v. Baltimore, 32 US 243 (1833).

[5] "The 1866 Civil Rights Act," Reconstruction: The Second Civil War, PBS, July 20, 2015; available at http://www.pbs.org/wgbh/amex/reconstruction/activism/ps_1866.html

[6] For instance, see Forrest McDonald, "Was the Fourteenth Amendment Constitutionally Adopted?" *Georgia Journal of Southern Legal History* Volume I, No. 1 (Spring/Summer 1991): 1-18. McDonald demonstrated that the ratification of the 14th Amendment was coercive, marred by "repeated irregularities" in the North's quest "to punish, plunder, and reconstruct the South." He concluded that the North would "march upon them and force them to adopt it at the point of a bayonet," making its adoption wholly illegitimate.

[7] Congressional Globe of the 39th Congress, 1st Session, 1866, 2883.

[8] Joseph James, *The Framing of the Fourteenth Amendment* (Chicago: University of Illinois Press, 1966), 161.

[9] Charles Fairman, "Does the Fourteenth Amendment Incorporate the Bill of Rights?" *Stanford Law Review* Volume 2, Number 1 (1949): 77.

[10] Raoul Berger, *Government by Judiciary: The Transformation of the Fourteenth Amendment*, Second Edition (Indianapolis: Liberty Fund, 1997), 173.

[11] Ibid, 171.

[12] Ibid.

[13] The Slaughter-House Cases, 83 US 36 (1873).

[14] Prudential Ins. Co v. Cheek, 259 US 543 (1922).

[15] Connecticut General Life Insurance Company v. Johnson, 303 US 77 (1938).

[16] Bartkus v. Illinois, 359 US 121 (1959).

[17] District of Columbia v. Heller, 554 US 570 (2008).

[18] For example, see Stephen Halbook, The Founders' Second Amendment: Origins of the Right to Bear Arms (Oakland: Independent Institute, 2008).

[19] "Former Justice Stevens: 14th Amendment Protects Gay Rights, Not Gun Rights," Breitbart.com, August 5, 2015; available at: http://www.breitbart.com/big-government/2015/08/05/former-justice-stevens-14th-amendment-protects-gay-rights-not-gun-rights/

[20] Opinion on the Constitutionality of a National Bank, in *Thomas Jefferson: Writings,* Edited by Merrill D. Peterson (New York: Viking Press, 1984), 416.

[21] Robert Bork, *The Tempting of America: The Political Seduction of the Law* (New York: Touchstone, 1990), 94.

[22] David Benner, *Compact of the Republic: The League of States and the Constitution* (Minneapolis: Life & Liberty Publishing Group, 2015), 286.

www.ingramcontent.com/pod-product-compliance
Lightning Source LLC
Chambersburg PA
CBHW060043040426
42331CB00032B/2255